T0014995

Kamala Harris

Vice President

by Elizabeth Neuenfeldt

BELLWETHER MEDIA • MINNEAPOLIS, MN

Blastoff! Readers are carefully developed by literacy experts to build reading stamina and move students toward fluency by combining standards-based content with developmentally appropriate text.

Level 1 provides the most support through repetition of high-frequency words, light text, predictable sentence patterns, and strong visual support.

Level 2 offers early readers a bit more challenge through varied sentences, increased text load, and text-supportive special features.

Level 3 advances early-fluent readers toward fluency through increased text load, less reliance on photos, advancing concepts, longer sentences, and more complex special features.

★ **Blastoff! Universe**

Reading Level

BLASTOFF! Beginners
Grade **K**

BLASTOFF! READERS
Grades **1–3**

BLASTOFF! DISCOVERY
Grade **4**

This edition first published in 2022 by Bellwether Media, Inc.

No part of this publication may be reproduced in whole or in part without written permission of the publisher. For information regarding permission, write to Bellwether Media, Inc., Attention: Permissions Department, 6012 Blue Circle Drive, Minnetonka, MN 55343.

Library of Congress Cataloging-in-Publication Data

Names: Neuenfeldt, Elizabeth, author.
Title: Kamala Harris : Vice President / by Elizabeth Neuenfeldt.
Description: Minneapolis, MN : Bellwether Media, Inc., 2022. | Series: Blastoff! Readers: Women leading the way | Includes index. | Audience: Ages 5-8 | Audience: Grades 2-3 | Summary: "Relevant images match informative text in this introduction to Kamala Harris. Intended for students in kindergarten through third grade"– Provided by publisher.
Identifiers: LCCN 2021041242 (print) | LCCN 2021041243 (ebook) | ISBN 9781644875957 (library binding) | ISBN 9781648346705 (paperback) | ISBN 9781648346064 (ebook)
Subjects: LCSH: Harris, Kamala, 1964–Juvenile literature. | Vice-presidents–United States–Biography–Juvenile literature. | Women lawyers–United States–Biography–Juvenile literature. | African American women lawyers–Biography–Juvenile literature. | Women legislators–United States–Biography–Juvenile literature. | African American women legislators–Biography–Juvenile literature.
Classification: LCC E901.1.H37 N49 2022 (print) | LCC E901.1.H37 (ebook) | DDC 973.934092 [B]–dc23
LC record available at https://lccn.loc.gov/2021041242
LC ebook record available at https://lccn.loc.gov/2021041243

Editor: Betsy Rathburn   Designer: Gabriel Hilger

Printed in the United States of America, North Mankato, MN.

Table of Contents

Who Is Kamala Harris?

Kamala Harris is the 49th vice president of the United States.

She is the first female, Black, and Asian American vice president!

Kamala becoming vice president

"BUT WHILE I MAY BE THE FIRST WOMAN IN THIS OFFICE, I WILL NOT BE THE LAST." (2020)

Kamala was born in 1964.
She first lived in California.
Then, her family moved
to Canada.

Oakland
Kamala's hometown

California

N
W E
S

Kamala and her mother, Shyamala

Her mom taught her about **civil rights**.

Getting Her Start

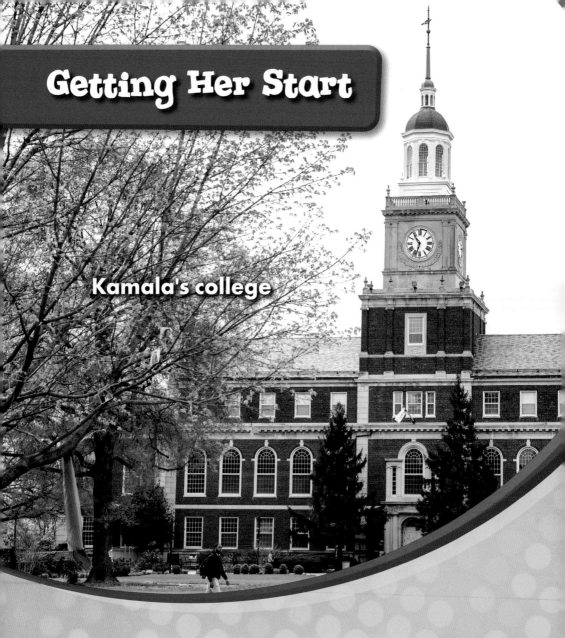

Kamala's college

Kamala moved back to the U.S. for college. She studied **politics**.

Then, she went to law school.
She wanted to help others.

Kamala Harris Profile

Birthday: October 20, 1964

Hometown: Oakland, California

Field: politics

Schooling: politics, law

Influences:
- **Shyamala Gopalan (mother)**
- **Shirley Chisholm (politician)**

In 2004, Kamala became a **district attorney**. She served in San Francisco, California.

Kamala introducing the Back on Track program

She helped form Back on Track. This program helps stop crimes.

Changing the World

In 2010, Kamala ran for **attorney general** of California. People did not think she would win.

Kamala proved them wrong. She won!

"ANYONE WHO CLAIMS TO BE A LEADER MUST SPEAK LIKE A LEADER. THAT MEANS SPEAKING WITH INTEGRITY AND TRUTH." (2019)

Kamala speaking at a civil rights event

Kamala worked hard as attorney general. She fought for online **privacy**. She fought for civil rights, too.

She also made a **database**. It helped Californians learn what crimes were happening.

Kamala Harris Timeline

2004	Kamala is the first woman of color to become the district attorney of San Francisco
2010	Kamala is elected to be the first female, Black, and Asian American attorney general of California
2015	Kamala forms an online database called OpenJustice
2017	Kamala becomes a U.S. senator
2021	Kamala begins her term as vice president of the U.S.

Kamala became a U.S. **senator** in 2017. She helped pass the **First Step Act**. It helped people in prisons.

Kamala becoming a senator

She also fought for the **DREAM Act**.
It helped **immigrants**.

Kamala's Future

Kamala with
President Joe Biden

In 2021, Kamala became the vice president! She works with President Joe Biden.

She helps people affected by the **COVID-19 pandemic**.

Kamala at a COVID-19 event

Kamala also fights for voting **rights**. She wants to end unfair voting laws.

She wants everyone to have a voice!

Kamala speaking about voting rights

"MY DAILY CHALLENGE TO MYSELF IS TO **BE PART OF THE** SOLUTION..." (2019)

Glossary

attorney general—the top lawyer in a state who represents the government in legal matters

civil rights—the rights that every person should have no matter their gender, race, religion, or identity

COVID-19 pandemic—an outbreak of the COVID-19 virus starting in December 2019 that led to millions of deaths and shutdowns around the world

database—a collection of information that is organized and stored by a computer

district attorney—a lawyer who represents a certain place in legal matters

DREAM Act—a law that helps some immigrants stay in the United States legally

First Step Act—a law that lowers punishments for prisoners and helps former prisoners avoid future crimes

immigrants—people who move from one country to another

politics—the activities related to governing

privacy—freedom from public attention

rights—things that every person should be allowed to have, get, or do

senator—a member of the Senate, a group that forms part of the United States Congress; it is a senator's job to make laws for the United States.

To Learn More

AT THE LIBRARY

Clinch, Shasta. *Kamala Is Speaking: Vice President for the People.* New York, N.Y.: Random House, 2021.

Hansen, Grace. *Kamala Harris: First Female Vice President of the United States.* Minneapolis, Minn.: Abdo Kids, 2021.

Rose, Rachel. *Kamala Harris: First Female Vice President.* Minneapolis, Minn.: Bearport Publishing Company, 2021.

ON THE WEB

FACTSURFER

Factsurfer.com gives you a safe, fun way to find more information.

1. Go to www.factsurfer.com.

2. Enter "Kamala Harris" into the search box and click 🔍.

3. Select your book cover to see a list of related content.

Index

The images in this book are reproduced through the courtesy of: Wikipedia, front cover (Kamala Harris), p. 9; Joseph Sohm, front cover (podium), pp. 3, 23; Alex Wong/ Getty Images, p. 4 (inset); Tasos Katopodis/ Stringer/ Getty Images , pp. 4-5; ARCHIVIO GBB/ Alamy, pp. 6-7; Kevin Sterling Scott, pp. 8-9; Stephen Dorian Miner, pp. 10-11 (bottom); Anne Cusack/ Getty Images, pp. 10-11 (top); Ralf-Finn Hestoft / Getty Images, p. 12 (inset); Sandy Huffaker/ Getty Images, pp. 12-13; Katie Falkenberg/ Getty Images, p. 14; Aaron P. Bernstein/ Stringer/ Getty Images, p. 16; Kevork Djansezian/ Stringer/ Getty Images, p. 17; American Photo Archive/ Alamy, pp. 18-19; Kent Nishimura/ Getty Images, p. 19; Sipa USA/ Alamy, p. 20 (inset); Stephen Maturen/ Stringer/ Getty Images, pp. 20-21.